FERGIE TIME

The funniest Sir Alex Ferguson quotes... ever!

by Gordon Law

Also available to buy

Copyright © 2017 by Gordon Law

No part of this publication may be reproduced, stored in a retrieval system or transmitted in any form by any means, electronic, mechanical, photocopying, or otherwise, without prior written permission of the publisher Gordon Law.

gordonlawauthor@yahoo.com

Printed in Europe and the USA
ISBN-13: 978-1981105748
ISBN-10: 1981105743

Photo courtesy of: Twocoms/Shutterstock.com

Contents

Introduction..4

Talking Balls..7

Best of Enemies...17

Can You Manage?..37

The Hairdryer...45

Media Circus..51

A Funny Old Game..73

Lifestyle Choice...83

Call the Manager...91

Ref Justice..101

Player Power..111

Fergie v Wenger...121

Say That Again...129

Introduction

Sir Alex Ferguson enjoyed the most successful managerial career in British history, reigning at Manchester United over four trophy-laden decades.

One of the greatest coaches ever, his tenure is defined by the incredible amount of silverware – including 13 Premier titles – secured while in the Old Trafford hot seat.

He not only built winning teams, was the master of mind games and famously influenced referees by gesturing to his watch for 'Fergie time' but was also known for his many memorable quotes.

Notorious for his 'hairdryer' treatment in the dressing room, the Scotsman rarely pulled his punches, either by blasting journalists or winding up his managerial counterparts.

None more so than Arsenal boss Arsene Wenger and the pair were locked in an on-going feud for many years as both teams slugged it out for the league crown.

Ferguson had a brilliant sense of humour too, from comic put-downs to pithy observations and strange philosophical musings, his colourful views grabbed everyone's attention.

Whether it was describing the pressure of the title run-in back in 2003 as "squeaky-bum time" or "knocking Liverpool off their perch" Fergie certainly had a way with words.

You'll find many of his funniest sound bites in this bumper collection, which also serves as a magnificent tribute to a football icon. Enjoy!

Gordon Law

FERGIE TIME

TALKING BALLS

THE FUNNIEST UNITED QUOTES... EVER!

"He'll be getting a hug and a kiss from me – maybe even two!"

Sir Alex Ferguson plans to reward Sam Allardyce after Bolton hold rivals Chelsea

"Gary Neville was having a piss one day, 45 yards away by a fence. Scholes whacked him right in the arse."

Fergie on Paul Scholes' shooting accuracy

"It was an incident which was freakish. If I tried it a hundred or a million times it could not happen again. If I could, I would have carried on playing [football]."

On kicking a boot that hit David Beckham

"[Andy] Cole should be scoring from those distances, but I'm not going to single him out."

He kinda does

"We're just taking care of an old man!"

On why veteran Paul Scholes didn't make the journey to Braga

"[Billy Bonds] was embarrassed that his team had played like Dervishes after being relegated. I know there is natural envy for Manchester United which often sees opponents raising their game but considering that the Hammers were bottom of the league, it was almost criminal."

Fergie fumes at the West Ham display

FERGIE TIME

"[Peter] Schmeichel was towering over me and the other players were covering their eyes. I was looking up and thinking, 'If he does hit me, I'm dead'."

He thanks his lucky stars after an argument with the giant Danish goalkeeper

"I kept saying, 'Will somebody please shoot Didier Drogba?'"

After Chelsea saw off United for the title in 2007

"The crowd were dead. It was like a funeral out there."

Fergie offers a blunt assessment

Talking Balls

"You know, he tried it about 10 minutes before he scored and I said to my assistant Brian Kidd, 'If he tries that again, he's off'."
On David Beckham's wonder goal against Wimbledon in 2008

"It's the best day since I got married."
The manager after a win at Sheffield United in 1992

"I can't believe it. I can't believe it. Football, bloody hell."
Fergie's memorable comments in his post-match interview after winning the 1999 Champions League trophy

FERGIE TIME

"At half-time it could have been 20-all! But common sense took over – or boring football took over!"
Ferguson on a 3-2 win over Fulham in 2005

"I've got a plan to stop him, it's called a machete. Plan B is a machine gun!"
On trying to handle former player Cristiano Ronaldo

"If we got that number of penalty kicks there would be an enquiry in the House of Commons."
Sir Alex plays mind games ahead of the clash against Man City, noting the number of penalties their rivals have won

Talking Balls

"We're dead lucky. We have only been doing it for 25 years."

A sarcastic Sir Alex replies to Roberto Mancini who reckons United have been lucky all season with their late comebacks

"He could have been killed."

After Ashley Williams fired a ball at Robin van Persie

"Rio didn't play because before the match he fell on his back, and Mikael Silvestre has felt his groin."

Sir Alex after United's game against the Kaizer Chiefs

FERGIE TIME

"All our players would acknowledge they were given a boost before a ball was kicked when our opponents turned up looking like a squad of bakers in cream-coloured suits. The sight gave our lads a great lift."

Fergie laughs at Liverpool's cup final suits

"You never know, malaria might hit the camp. We've got to hope something like that happens."

On United trying to make up ground on Chelsea's 13-point lead

"It was particularly pleasing that our goalscorers scored tonight."

Tautology from Sir Alex

Talking Balls

"[Wayne] Rooney is from Liverpool and everyone from that city has a chip on their shoulder. So if an injustice is done to him on the pitch of course he is going to react."

He defends Rooney after he was sent off for sarcastically applauding a referee's decision

"He went into that cauldron as calmly as someone popping round the corner for a newspaper."

On the Paul Scholes winner against Inter in the 1999 Champions League quarter-final

"It hurts, badly. Suicide is the only way to describe our defeat."

After a 5-1 loss at Manchester City in 1989

FERGIE TIME

BEST OF ENEMIES

FERGIE TIME

"Maybe they will get some joy from it and realise how important we are to England instead of treating us like sh*t."

Sir Alex barbs at the FA after eight United players were called up to the England squad

"He's a bully, a f*cking big-time Charlie."

On his former player Paul Ince, now at Liverpool

"You scumbag, you ratbag, you dirty b*stard."

Fergie lets rip at Feyenoord's Paul Bosvelt after a rash challenge on Denis Irwin

Best of Enemies

"They give the impression that lynching would be too good for us."
On Leeds United

"What made it really obscene was that Madrid, as General Franco's club, had a history of being able to get whoever and whatever they wanted, before democracy came to Spain."
Fergie is bitter at Real Madrid over Cristiano Ronaldo

"I wouldn't want to expose my back to him in a hurry."
He's not a friend of Gordon Strachan

FERGIE TIME

"Do you think I would enter into a contract with that mob? Absolutely no chance. I would not sell them a virus. That is a 'no' by the way. There is no agreement whatsoever between the clubs."

When asked if it was true that Cristiano Ronaldo was set to join Real Madrid

"I think you should respect a manager. I don't think you'd ever get me doing something like that – you won't. You have to have humility. But he is beyond the pale."

Ferguson attacks Rafa Benitez for allegedly disrespecting Sam Allardyce

Best of Enemies

"They got him sent off, everyone sprinted towards the referee – typical Germans."

He accuses Bayern Munich's players of urging the referee to show Rafael a red card

"Our programme didn't do us any favours and I think we have been handicapped by the Premier League in the fixture list. They tell me it's not planned. Bloody hell!"

Sir Alex fumes at the fixture pile-up

"Don't swap shirts with those dirty b*stards."

Fergie hits out at Champions League opponents Feyenoord

FERGIE TIME

"We will only be in trouble if we listen to Jose too much."

After Jose Mourinho said United "would be in trouble" if they thought the league was won in December 2006

"My greatest challenge is not what's happening at the moment, my greatest challenge was knocking Liverpool right off their f*cking perch. And you can print that."

One of Fergie's greatest lines

"Dennis Wise could start a fight in an empty house."

His view on the firebrand midfielder

Best of Enemies

"Liverpool-Manchester United games are fantastic. It doesn't matter if you were playing tiddlywinks, it would be really competitive."

On the North West derby

"Real have no morals at all. They think they can ride roughshod over everyone but they won't do it with us. In terms of great clubs, Barcelona have far better moral issues than Real Madrid will ever have."

Sir Alex hits out at Real Madrid again

"We all know about the Doc. He is what he is, a bitter old man."

On pundit Tommy Docherty

FERGIE TIME

"It's City isn't it? They are a small club with a small mentality. All they can talk about is Manchester United. They can't get away from it. They think taking Tevez away from Manchester United is a triumph. It is poor stuff."

Sir Alex on that Carlos Tevez poster

"Sometimes you have a noisy neighbour. You cannot do anything about that. They will always be noisy. You just have to get on with your life, put your television on and turn it up a bit louder."

Fergie on United's Manchester rivals

Best of Enemies

"His football club have been involved in so many things about referees over the years. It seems to me that, if you contest something at Chelsea and they don't get their own way, then something happens. Either referees or players are threatened and things like that. It's an incredible club. I think he should button his lip now for the rest of the season. I may be only just beginning because there is plenty for me to talk about with Jose and referees, and Chelsea and referees. I've got a catalogue of them, a big file, in my office if you want me to bring it out. But we'll leave that for another day."

He responds to Chelsea manager Jose Mourinho who reckons United get better treatment from referees

FERGIE TIME

"Has any chairman since Mao had more faith in his own opinions than Ken Bates? If laying down the law was an Olympic sport, the Chelsea chief would be staggering under the weight of gold medals."

Sir Alex on the former Chelsea and Leeds supremo

"They could buy every player in the world, but can they buy a team? Can they buy a Manchester United spirit? The problem with all that money is that you buy indiscriminately. Sunderland in the 1950s, the Bank of England team. Relegated."

Fergie dismisses City's hopes of success

Best of Enemies

"What the f*ck are you lot playing at? That is the biggest load of sh*t I've ever seen. Not one of you can look me in the eye, because not one of you deserves to have a say. I can't believe you've come here and decided to toss it off like that c*nt you're playing out there."

He unleashes the hairdryer at half-time against Sheffield Wednesday

"You could never tell what these people are doing. Even if I was sitting having breakfast with them I would not know what they were thinking."

On the FA who decided to ban Patrice Evra for four games after he confronted a Chelsea groundsman

FERGIE TIME

"They are the worst losers of all time. They don't know how to lose. Maybe it's just Manchester United. They don't lose many games to other teams."
Sir Alex hits out at Arsenal

"When you think about the history that Liverpool have got, Chelsea don't compare."
Fergie takes a swipe at rivals Chelsea

"I reckon that comment goes alongside his claim a few years ago that you don't win anything with youngsters."
Fergie blasts Alan Hansen who claimed United have not played well for 18 months

"Rival United? Arsenal? Never! They will need three stadiums and 33 teams to rival us as a club. Nobody is as big as Manchester United. Nobody will ever be either."

Fergie on the Gunners

"It's a dysfunctional unit. I don't think they know what they are doing, but it will always be that way."

On the FA's disciplinary committee

"All this 'Guvnor' nonsense should have been left in his toy box."

Referring to Paul Ince's nickname

FERGIE TIME

"Pardew has come out and criticised me. He is the worst at haranguing referees. He shoves them and makes a joke of it. How he can criticise me is unbelievable. He forgets the help I gave him, by the way."

Sir Alex on Newcastle's Alan Pardew

"I hope that before I die, someone can explain the 'West Ham way'. What is it? They last won a trophy in 1980, the FA Cup. I never played against any West Ham team that played football I was afraid of. They were always surviving, or lucky as hell against us."

Fergie doesn't understand the mystique around West Ham's style of play

Best of Enemies

"You must be joking. Do I look as if I'm a masochist ready to cut myself? How does relegation sound instead?"

After reporters asked if Liverpool were real title contenders

"Arsenal's big advantage is that they can play Pat Rice at right-back and Arsene at centre forward on Saturday."

Ferguson on Arsenal resting players ahead of their 2009 Champions League semi-final against United

"He has no respect for anyone but himself."

Fergie on Jose Mourinho in 2007

FERGIE TIME

"I think he was an angry man. He must have been disturbed for some reason. I think you have got to cut through the venom of it and hopefully he'll reflect and understand what he said was absolutely ridiculous."

On Rafa Benitez's memorable 'fact' rant

"Weird. I really don't know what he was talking about. He'd obviously worked himself up into something, because he was reading it out."

Fergie continues

"I would need to read more of Freud before I could really understand all that."

And more reaction

"There are one or two football agents I simply do not like. And Mino Raiola, Paul Pogba's agent, is one of them."

Fair to say that Ferguson is not a fan of Paul Pogba's agent

"I read that Scolari is more experienced than me. What have I been doing for the last 34 years? I must have missed something or been asleep somewhere. They are saying because of Scolari's experience, Chelsea are going to win the league. I don't understand that."

Sir Alex on new Chelsea manager 'Big' Phil Scolari

"I know what it's going to be in the next round – us against Chelsea. I'm going down to Soho Square to check those balls."

Ferguson makes his prediction for the FA Cup draw

"It'll take them a century to get to our level of history."

Sir Alex mocks Premier League champions Manchester City

Reporter: "Do you know how many managers City have had in your 25 years with United?"
Ferguson: "Fourteen, but I wish it was 15."
Fergie takes a swipe at Roberto Mancini

Best of Enemies

"It is nonsense. Why would I refuse to shake his hand? I was signing autographs and I never saw him. Why he has said that I have no idea. If he wanted to shake hands he could have stood straight in front of me. It is absolute nonsense."

On claims by Chelsea interim manager Rafael Benitez that he refused to shake hands

"We can bring Keane back if he wants and make it interesting."

Sir Alex warns Patrick Vieira he might re-sign old foe Roy Keane if he continues with his negative United comments

FERGIE TIME

CAN YOU MANAGE?

FERGIE TIME

"If footballers think they are above the manager's control, there is only one word to say: 'Goodbye'."

There is only one man in charge

"I was close to putting my head in the oven as I have ever been, and I think there would have been plenty of volunteers to turn on the gas."

Fergie feels the pressure during his early days as boss

"The one thing you need in this game is earplugs."

Speaking about Arsene Wenger's critics

Can You Manage?

"I asked [Paul Ince] why he got so upset when someone called him black. After all, he frequently referred to me as a Scottish so-and-so, so what was the difference? He told me the Scots aren't a race. Naturally, I had to remind him that we are in fact the master race."

Fergie is the boss

"People get carried away and use superlatives such as 'fantastic' and 'wonderful'. I just minimise it to 'well done'. I think they're two fantastic words."

Sir Alex keeps his players grounded

FERGIE TIME

"They will wait until the last minute while I'm on the bench having three heart attacks and contorted with stomach pains."

On his players making him sweat before coming up with late goals to decide games

"Coming up the stairs at Old Trafford recently, a young player, one of the 16-year-olds called me 'Alex'. I said, 'Were you at school with me?' He said, 'No'. I said, 'Well call me Mr Ferguson or Boss'. Some of the senior players were drawing desperate faces. They were thinking, 'He'll kill him!'"

It's all about respect for Fergie

Can You Manage?

"I remember going to see Andrea Bocelli, the opera singer. I had never been to a classical concert in my life. But I am watching this and thinking about the co-ordination and the teamwork."

The manager is always learning

"The only advice I can give to you is don't let the players take the Mickey out of you."

His advice to new boss Paul Ince

"So you can get another job – become a milkman!"

He says his wife Cathy won't let him retire

FERGIE TIME

"Every time somebody looks at me I feel I have betrayed that man. You feel as if you have to sneak around corners, feel as if you are some kind of criminal."

Fergie is under pressure in the late 80s

Ferguson: "Five hours' sleep is all I need."
Reporter: "Like Margaret Thatcher?"
Ferguson: "Don't associate me with that woman."

"They think of United and just burst out laughing. I feel like jumping down the phone and belting them one. It's that frustrating."

On speaking with managers to buy players with little money in 1987

Can You Manage?

"You go into it because it's in the blood. I remember Viv Anderson saying to me that you had to be off your head to want to be a manager. Then I was in the car one day and it came on the radio that Barnsley had appointed Viv as manager. I gave him a call straight away and said, 'Who's off their head now?"

On the addiction of management

"I remember Jock Stein saying, 'Always wait until Monday [to talk to players] so you can give a studied response to a match'. But I couldn't do that to save my life."

Sir Alex is impatient

FERGIE TIME

THE HAIRDRYER

FERGIE TIME

"That was Mark Hughes who invented [the hairdryer] phrase. After he left me, of course."

"Throwing tea cups? That only happened once or twice."

"Sometimes I wish it had been with somebody 6ft 10. Sometimes it's a small guy, sometimes it's a medium-sized guy. I've no discrimination that way. Sometimes there's guilt. Sometimes you say to yourself, 'Why did I do that?'."

"[Harry Redknapp] is never in a tizzy – unlike myself."

The Hairdryer

"I don't like losing but I've mellowed. I maybe have a short fuse but it goes away quicker now."

"Myths grow all the time. If I was to listen to the number of times I've thrown teacups then we've gone through some crockery in this place. It's completely exaggerated, but I don't like people arguing back with me."

"There's nothing wrong with losing your temper, if it is for the right reasons."

"I'm a pussy cat now, too old to lose my temper."

FERGIE TIME

"Sometimes I lose my temper, sometimes I don't. If someone argues with me I have to win the argument. So I start heading towards them, that's where the hairdryer comes in. I can't lose an argument. The manager can never lose an argument."

"I came in, there was this big tea urn and I went to smash it. And I'm not kidding you, I nearly broke my arm. I kicked the tray so hard the cups went up over the wall. Archie Knox, my assistant, was sitting there with tea running down the back of his tracksuit."

The Hairdryer

"If it's in your nature to lose your temper, let it out. Don't keep it bottled up otherwise you end up growling and kicking doors and not getting across what you actually feel. I've thrown more tea cups across the dressing room than I can tell you. But as far as I'm concerned, anger is not a problem. Losing your temper is OK."

"People must recognise that I am not the three-headed monster that I have been portrayed. I've got feelings just like everyone else."

FERGIE TIME

MEDIA CIRCUS

FERGIE TIME

"I should have recognised that voice. Hearing it is like having poison creep all over my body."
Sir Alex to a Daily Mirror reporter

"You lot had me out of the door three years ago. You had me in a bath-chair down on Torquay beach."
Ferguson, speaking to the media in 1999

"You've enthralled me all season with your honesty, integrity – and nonsense!"
Fergie's sarcasm. One journalist retorted: "Likewise!"

Media Circus

"If you ever predict my team right, I'll give you a free weekend up in Loch Lomond. And I'll make sure the midges are out for you."
Sir Alex's somewhat kind offer

"When you shake hands with the devil you have to pay the price. Television is God at the moment. When the fixtures come out, they can pick and choose because they want the big teams on TV."
He hits out at the TV companies

FERGIE TIME

"There are members of the London press who seek to antagonise me, deliberately."
Sir Alex is not happy

"I love you all – I've come to spread peace!"
He addresses the media before the 2008 Champions League triumph

"Struggling. Are you serious? We're not struggling."
When asked by a reporter if United were struggling in the Champions League after their 2-2 draw with Benfica in 2011. He then storms out of the room

Media Circus

"Jesus Christ. How do you lot come up with this stuff? It's Korky the Cat, Dennis the Menace stuff. Do you read Lord Snooty? Which comic is it you guys work for these days?"

When asked about his possible interest in Darren Bent

"They [the press] have a hatred of Manchester United. It's always been there. It goes with the territory."

Ferguson's rant before ending his press conference after just 74 seconds

"I'm not f*cking talking to you. He's a f*cking great player. Yous are f*cking idiots."
To journalists who criticised Juan Sebastian Veron

"I don't know why you ask these questions, you're just looking for stupid little things."
Sir Alex gives TV reporter Kelly Cates a blasting

"I'm here to discuss Manchester United, not one player. You want a headline, I want a team performance."
Fergie gives it straight

Media Circus

"The press have had a field day. The only person they have not spoken to is Barack Obama because he is busy. It is unfortunate but I am the manager of the most famous club in the world. Not Newcastle, a wee club in the North East. I was demonstrative. I am always demonstrative. Everyone knows that. I am an emotional guy but I was not abusive."

Ferguson rants about Alan Pardew

"I wouldn't want to blunt your imagination with the facts."

He mocks the journalists in the room

FERGIE TIME

"As I have said time and time again, the only thing that determines my staying here is my health and unfortunately for you lot [the media], I'm in rude health! So you'll be left to suffer me for many more years. You'll be gone before I'm gone, don't you worry!"

Sir Alex scoffs at claims that he is set to retire

"The BBC are dying for us to lose. Everyone is from Liverpool with a supporter's badge. They will be at our games every week until we lose, that mob, Bob, Barry, Hansen, the lot of them."

Fergie feels the BBC's pundits have a Liverpool bias

Media Circus

"It's Jose, he's panicking already."

Fergie cracks a joke after his mobile rings during a media conference

"You won't believe it, he is a Chelsea fan – sad man."

The Scot reacts after the phone rings again. He had only been given it earlier that day and couldn't switch it off

"I have banned two papers from the press conferences and they won't get back in here until they apologise."

He is not happy about stories written that he has had a fall-out with Wayne Rooney

FERGIE TIME

"I don't know what you're talking about. I think that'll do us there."

Fergie puts an end to a press conference after a reporter asks that if players are fearful of him, then what scares him

"Jimmy Hill is verbal when it suits him. If there's a prat going about in this world, he is the prat. He writes us off in the warm-up, that's how much he knows about the game."

The manager has a go at the pundit after he criticises Eric Cantona

Media Circus

"You want a f*cking story as usual... Your f*cking stuff is a disgrace to journalism and you are. The stuff you f*cking come out with..."

Fergie likes to use the 'f' word

"Some of the ex-player, ex-manager pundits are the worst. It's a disgrace the way they sit there criticising guys they used to play with, just to make a bit of impact."

He doesn't like the criticism

"The journalists call this place Colditz. That's right. And that's just the way I like it."

On United's new Carrington training ground

FERGIE TIME

"You've no right to ask me that question John. You're out of order... You know fine well my ruling on that. Right, that's the interview finished... I'm going to cancel that interview, the whole f*cking lot of it. Cancel it, right? F*cking make sure that does not go out, John."

Fergie blasts John Motson in 1995 after he questioned Roy Keane's disciplinary record

"This is a press conference about a bloody football match. I'm not answering that. Christ."

Sir Alex fumes at a reporter who asked him about the Ryder Cup

Media Circus

"Did you know that in 1999 they picked David Ginola for the Football Writers' award? Ginola! We won the treble that year. In fact, the only thing we didn't win was the Boat Race – and they still gave it to Ginola. Can you believe that?"

He tells it how it is to an overseas reporter

"That's absolute b*llocks, that. Absolute nonsense."

Fergie slams a TV reporter who asked if the defeat to Chelsea the previous week was the worst of his United career

FERGIE TIME

"All of us associated with the team were blissfully demented. Gary Newbon tried to interview me for television and, I am sure, got a flood of gibberish for his pains. I didn't mind sounding like an idiot though. There was no happier idiot on the planet."

Ferguson looks back on his famous post-Champions League TV interview

"Do you know that the most perfect English in the world is spoken in Scotland? That's absolutely correct by the way. If you want to go up to Inverness for a day, you will learn how to speak English perfectly."

Fergie explains to a foreign journalist

Media Circus

"Have you seen our fixtures list? If you had, you wouldn't even ask that question. You have no idea. No idea at all. That's it, it's all over. You can all f*ck off, the lot of you."

When asked why he couldn't put out a youth side in the FA Cup instead of withdrawing to play in the 1999 FIFA Club World Cup

"I don't want to go anywhere. I'm enjoying the company of you gentlemen too much. Now... mark me down as liar of the year."

When the press asked about retirement in 2007

FERGIE TIME

"I don't know anyone in the game who has any time for Emlyn Hughes. He is a disappointing character and it is sad that a man who has achieved so much in the game can resort to gutter journalism."

On the former Liverpool player-turned pundit

"Jesus Christ! Do they get them straight from school these days!"

Sir Alex to a journalist who was in his 30s

"Never try to read the mind of a madman!"

Fergie to reporters speculating on his team

Media Circus

"I don't give any of you credibility, do you know that? You talk about wanting to have an association with people here and you wonder why I don't get on with you? But you're a f*cking embarrassment, a real embarrassment. One of these days the door is going to shut on you permanently."

The media get a roasting

"That's a good question. But it would take a whole interview to get it and that's an interview you're never going to f*cking get."

On being asked about United's poor season

FERGIE TIME

"I get the papers every morning and I have a good laugh about them, I get my cup of tea. I look at what you've written. I get an aspirin to make sure I get over it. And then I get over it. And then I go about my day's work still laughing."

Sir Alex sees the lighter side

Dean Morse: "Is there any way to improve the relationship between the newspaper and the club?"

Ferguson: "Yes, you can f*ck off and die."

The Daily Mirror sports editor tries to reconcile with Fergie

Media Circus

"There have been times when I have not agreed with what people have written, and when you write positive things I tend to dismiss them. I've never held a grudge. It's not my style."

The manager makes his point

"You can't accuse footballers of failing society. They are very kind, going to hospitals and seeing kids, but in the main the press don't seem to want to write a good word about them."

He thinks they are harsh on players

FERGIE TIME

"Mice? I don't know about mice but we've got a bloody big problem with rats. And you walked right into that one, son."

Fergie ribs a journalist who asked about mice on the Old Trafford pitch

"None of your business! Do I ask if you're still going to those f*cking gays clubs?"

The Scot lashes out at a journalist who enquired if he's going to the World Cup

"That's you finished at this club."

Fergie to a TV reporter who asked about Roy Keane's criticism of his teammates

Media Circus

"Bayern Munich have a press conference every bloody day. Christ, can you imagine it? I have to summon up every ounce of energy to do it once a week."

He doesn't enjoy facing the media

"I remember Gary Lineker, a bright boy from the BBC... says I'm childish. Well, he should know about that himself."

On his feud with the BBC

"You f*cking sell your papers and radio shows off the back of this club."

Another rant at the members of the press

FERGIE TIME

A FUNNY OLD GAME

FERGIE TIME

"I am sure to get my usual great reception at Celtic. Maybe I will stand in the centre-circle this time to get the full applause."

The former Rangers player ahead of United's Champions League match at Celtic Park

"Have you seen the last six World Cups? It is better going to the dentist I suppose."

Sir Alex is not excited about the tournament

"Gianfranco Zola once sent Gary Pallister the wrong way to such an extent that he needed a ticket to get back in."

Zola is a player he regrets not signing

A Funny Old Game

"England do not have a game until February, so why make a decision over a bacon butty at 8.30am?"
On the FA sacking England boss Steve McClaren

"Give me Zidane and 10 pieces of wood, and I will win you the Champions League."
Ferguson was a big fan of the Frenchman

"He said, 'Garth Crooks and I have an understanding'. I said, 'Have you? Aye, it's a good one. He's scoring goals and you're messing around in the middle of the park'."
Fergie tells Steve Archibald how it is

FERGIE TIME

"See this man? Neither of you two will ever be good enough to lace his boots. Go and get him some toast."

Fergie to Wayne Rooney and Ryan Giggs when the Man City legend Ken Barnes came to United's training ground

"They come out with the 'English are so strong, we're terrible in the air, we can't do this, we can't do that'. Then they beat you 3-0."

On Italian flattery

"He was a magician on the park. He could have put a size-five football in an egg cup."

On Jim Baxter

A Funny Old Game

"I remember some years ago I asked a young player if he had heard of Denis Law and he said he hadn't. So I shot him."

Great players must be respected

"Jose is very intelligent, he has charisma, his players play for him and he is a good looking guy. I think I have most of those things too, apart from his good looks."

On Jose Mourinho

"The only team I look out for now is Benburb, my local junior team."

Fergie remembers his roots

FERGIE TIME

"He was certainly full of it, calling me 'Boss' and 'Big Man' when we had our post-match drink after the first leg. But it would help if his greetings were accompanied by a decent glass of wine. What he gave me was paint stripper."
On Inter Milan manager Jose Mourinho

"Brian Clough provided ample proof that he was one of British football's greatest managers. That he was almost certainly its rudest is perhaps another distinction he is proud to claim. He is welcome to it."
On the legendary Nottingham Forest manager

A Funny Old Game

"Gareth Southgate is very naive. He's just a young manager. We'll have to give him a chance to settle in."

Reacting to the Middlesbrough manager's claims that Cristiano Ronaldo was a diver

"Some players cry now in the dressing room. Bryan Robson never used to cry."

Fergie bemoans players' lack of character

"On top of all his other advantages, he is such a good-looking b*stard he makes most of us look like Bela Lugosi."

On former Italy boss Marcello Lippi

FERGIE TIME

"Patrick would love to have come here last year, but they wouldn't let him. Players always want to play for a bigger club."

On trying to sign Arsenal captain Patrick Vieira

"One thousand games in purgatory, eh?"

Fergie on handing Dave Bassett an award for 1,000 games as manager

"Whether he's getting too old, I don't know. But things can happen to people in power. Look at some of the despots in Africa."

The manager on FIFA's president Sepp Blatter

"I like Jose. I think he sees himself as the young gunslinger who has come into town to challenge the sheriff who has been around for a while. He has a great sense of humour and there is a devilish wit about him. Don't believe everything you read about mind games. We get on."

Fergie on the then-Chelsea boss

"His career flew on gossamer wings. But he also gave me the impression that if he didn't get his own way he was liable to pick up his ball and go home."

On Kevin Keegan's fragile temperament

FERGIE TIME

LIFESTYLE CHOICE

FERGIE TIME

"His life changed when he met his wife. She's in pop and David got another image. He's developed this 'fashion thing'."

On David Beckham meeting the Spice Girl Victoria

"Now that Jose [Mourinho] has gone I don't know what I'm going to do with my wine."

Sir Alex now has more booze

"They are cocooned by their parents, they need to be seen with their tattoos and earrings. Some even cry in the dressing room."

On the modern footballer

Lifestyle Choice

"You can't beat Sinatra. I was actually supposed to have dinner with him one night, but we lost to Charlton so I cancelled it and went home!"

Ferguson the bad loser

"I told her I had a match but she wasn't having any of it. She said it was a friendly and that I had to help her to pack because we're moving house."

On wife Cathy stopping him going to a game

"At 68, when you go to sleep at night, all you want to do is wake up in the morning."

Sir Alex is feeling his age

FERGIE TIME

"That wife of mine just bullies me. She throws me out of the door at seven o'clock every morning! So that's a definite no. Oh no, I dare not risk the wrath of that lass from the Gorbals."

Ferguson claims that it's his wife Cathy who stops him from retiring

"Apparently I'm allowed to hang my washing on Glasgow Green, which is an interesting one. And if I ever get arrested in the city, I'm entitled to my own cell, which could come in handy at some point."

After being made freeman of Glasgow

Lifestyle Choice

"My wife cringes every time someone calls me 'Sir Alex' or calls her 'Lady Cathy'. She says, 'I don't know why you accepted it in the first place'."

His wife is down-to-earth

"Could I not have two bullets?"

When asked if he had a bullet in a gun, would he use it on Arsene Wenger or Victoria Beckham

"He was never a problem until he got married."

Sir Alex on David Beckham

FERGIE TIME

"We go to the cinema almost every week. Cathy and I go to the early show at around five o'clock. I get my pick 'n' mix and my hot dog and ice cream, Cathy says I'm a pig."

On date nights with the wife

"You'll never guess what Beckham wore to training today. He had this bloody spingly, spangly tracksuit on – he looked like Gary Glitter."

Fergie on Becks' fashion sense

"I am such a bloody talented guy. I might go into painting or something like that."

He's just so modest

Lifestyle Choice

"I found him unreachable. Time and again I would have him in my office, attempting to bring home to him the danger that alcohol was doing to his life. He would sit there and just nod in agreement, then walk out the door and carry on as before."

On trying to help Paul McGrath

"I once forgot to get her a Christmas present. I remembered on Christmas Eve and pressed the panic button but it was too late – the shops were shut. So I slipped a cheque in with her card on Christmas Day. Another bummer idea... she tore it in two and dropped it in the bin."

Fergie knows the real boss

FERGIE TIME

CALL THE MANAGER

FERGIE TIME

"Portsmouth's away dressing room is not great and the one at Craven Cottage is smaller than my office. Fulham is one of my favourite grounds but when you have 18 players stripping down, plus coaches, physios and kit men, it is ridiculous really."

Fergie on football's changing rooms

"I had to get rid of this idea that Manchester United were a drinking club, rather than a football club."

He had to tackle big issues with Norman Whiteside and Paul McGrath

"It's getting tickly now – squeaky-bum time, I call it. It's going to be an interesting few weeks and the standard of the Premiership is such that nothing will be easy."

Sir Alex's now world-famous expression to describe the pressure of the title run-in in 2003

"You would have thought that I had left 11 corpses on the steps of a funeral home."

Ferguson did not take kindly to suggestions that he left successor David Moyes with a bad set of players after retiring

FERGIE TIME

"I don't care what I win it by. It could be a dodgy goal off someone's backside. "

Sir Alex isn't fussed at how United win the league title

"Of course I would prefer to be facing Brechin in the final, with the greatest of respect to them."

On his ideal opponents in the 2011 Champions League showpiece

"Get yourself down to the library and read a book."

He'd rather his players stayed off Twitter

Call the Manager

"One of these days, they are going to come up the stairs from their dressing room and find a bloody big padlock on the treatment room door."

Fergie is fed up with players spending too much time in the injury room

"Sometimes I feel I have known nearly as many scouts as [Robert] Baden-Powell."

Reflecting on his years in the game

"It's interesting that the games in which we've dropped points are those where we've failed to score."

Fergie the rocket scientist

FERGIE TIME

"Blackburn will have to finish like Devon Loch to give us any chance."

On fighting for the league crown with Rovers in 1994/95

"That whole experience was more painful than my hip replacement."

On negotiating the signing of Dimitar Berbatov with Tottenham chairman Daniel Levy in 2008

"Eleven Nobel laureates are not going to win the FA Cup."

Ferguson looks for heart in his players, not just talent

"When we won the league, I came out of the dressing room and I said, 'I've written three names, put them in an envelope. Those are the three players who are going to let us down next season'."

Ferguson after winning the Premier League title in 1993

"We had a virus that infected everyone at United. It was called winning."

Not a bad virus to have!

"We had a good record until Jose [Mourinho] came along and spoiled the party."

Sir Alex no longer enjoys trips to Chelsea

"It's strange for a country like Holland to call us arrogant. You are not short of it yourself."
Addressing a Dutch reporter who claimed he was being complacent for resting some players in a 3-1 defeat to PSV Eindhoven

"It is totally out of the question. There is no way we would sell him, or any of our best players."
Shortly before selling David Beckham to Real Madrid

"The 1994 team had mental toughness. So many of them. Real tough b*stards."
Fergie remembers a team of real men

Call the Manager

"There wasn't even a squirrel applauding me, but it didn't matter because we were champions."

On hearing that Oldham had beaten rivals Aston Villa while on a golf course to secure the 1993 title

"What youth policy? He's left me a shower of sh*t."

On former manager Ron Atkinson's legacy

"One of my players would have to be hit by an axe to get a penalty at the moment."

Sir Alex is hard done by

FERGIE TIME

REF JUSTICE

FERGIE TIME

"I cannot believe the decision [of the referee]. Okay, it is human error, but it was one of the worst in my lifetime."

After Darren Fletcher was booked for diving in a game against CSKA Moscow

"Everyone knows that for us to get awarded a penalty we need a certificate from the Pope and a personal letter from the Queen."

Fergie slams the referee after Leeds were awarded a spot kick

"I didn't expect him [Gerrard] to be charged, simply because it is a dysfunctional unit at the FA. I don't think they know what they are doing... but I certainly think if he was a Manchester United player he would have been done – as was the case with Rio Ferdinand."

On Steven Gerrard escaping punishment for an alleged elbow on Portsmouth's Michael Brown

"It was the 95th minute of their usual seven minutes of injury time."

After a late Arsenal equaliser in 2008

FERGIE TIME

"The pace of the game demanded a referee who was fit. It is an indictment of our game. You see referees abroad who are as fit as butcher's dogs. We have some who are fit. He wasn't fit. He was taking 30 seconds to book a player. He was needing a rest. It was ridiculous."

Sir Alex on referee Alan Wiley

"I felt for a while as if I was watching Australian rules!"

Fergie hits out at ref Alan Wiley after United's 1-1 draw at Everton

Ref Justice

"Cristiano [Ronaldo]. Why would he want to go down? He was on a hat-trick, he had gone round the keeper and was brought down. It was a ridiculous decision."

The manager is not a happy chap after a penalty award is turned down

"It is the only industry where you can't tell the truth."

After the FA handed him a five-match touchline ban for criticising referee Martin Atkinson following a defeat by Chelsea in 2011

FERGIE TIME

"Have we got a supply of Mogadon?"

Fergie after hearing that German referee Herbert Fandel was to officiate their next Champions League tie

"Can anyone tell me why they give referees a watch? It's certainly not for keeping the time."

On ref Graham Poll who added just three minutes of stoppage time against Everton

"We will not let this man deny us the title."

On referee David Elleray showing Denis Irwin a red card against Liverpool in 1999

Ref Justice

"They gave us four minutes [injury time], that's an insult to the game. It denies you a proper chance to win a football match. There were six substitutions, the trainer came on, so that's four minutes right away and the goalkeeper must have wasted about two or three minutes and they took their time at every goal kick. That's obvious to everyone today and it's a flaw in the game that the referee is responsible for time keeping. It's ridiculous that it's 2012 and the referee still has control of that."

Ferguson after losing 3-2 at home to Tottenham Hotspur

FERGIE TIME

"A lot of managers have to leave here choking on their own sick, biting their tongue, afraid to tell the truth."

Fergie fumes at bad officiating during a 3-3 draw at Liverpool in 1988

"Rafa [Benitez] is trying to get the referee on his side. He must think we are bloody stupid."

Sir Alex on his rival manager

"You lose your faith in the refereeing sometimes... it was a bad one."

Fergie isn't happy after a loss at Chelsea

Ref Justice

"This atmosphere is hard to handle for a ref. Whether he had enough experience or not, I don't know."

Ferguson on Andre Marriner's display at Liverpool

"Some referees don't like it. They don't like the truth. But I just told him how bad he was in the first half."

He makes his feelings clear to referee Mark Clattenburg

"You can't applaud a referee."

Sir Alex makes a fair point

FERGIE TIME

PLAYER POWER

FERGIE TIME

"If he was an inch taller he'd be the best centre half in Britain. His father is 6ft 2in – I'd check the milkman."

Ferguson on Gary Neville

"When a player is at his peak, he feels as if he can climb Everest in his slippers."

Sir Alex on Paul Ince

"I remember my shock and awe seeing Dion Dublin coming out of the shower. I mean, it was just magnificent."

Referring to Dion Dublin's manhood

Player Power

"He's had two cruciates and a broken ankle. That's not easy. Every player attached to the club is praying the boy gets a break."

A break? Fergie on Wes Brown

"Here at Old Trafford, they reckon Bestie had double-jointed ankles."

On George Best

"Nicky Butt's a real Manchester boy. A bit of a scallywag. He comes from Gorton where it is said they take the pavements in of a night time."

On his midfielder

FERGIE TIME

"He was 13 and just floated over the ground like a cocker spaniel chasing a piece of silver paper in the wind."

Ferguson recalls the first time he saw Ryan Giggs play

"He has the most savage tongue you can imagine. He can debilitate the most confident person in the world in seconds with that tongue"

Sir Alex on Roy Keane

"Eric Cantona couldn't tackle a fish supper."

On the Frenchman's weakness

Player Power

"Mark Bosnich was a terrible professional. We played down at Wimbledon and Bosnich was tucking into everything: sandwiches, soups, steaks. He was going through the menu. I told him, 'For Christ's sake, Mark, we've got the weight off you. Why are you tucking into all that stuff?' We arrived back in Manchester and Mark was on [his] mobile phone to a Chinese restaurant to order a takeaway. Is there no end to you? I just couldn't make an impact on him."

Fergie on the former goalkeeper

"At 38 years of age… or is he 39? Maybe 40, I don't know."

Sir Alex forgets how old Ryan Giggs is

FERGIE TIME

"The biggest ego came with beautiful vanity, with that fantastic body of his. Ronaldo would stand in the mirror and the others would throw socks and jock straps at him!"

Ferguson on Cristiano Ronaldo's ego

"I used to get a letter from a supporter saying I was off my head because I wasn't playing Steve Bruce at centre forward, although in fairness it was probably Brucie writing it himself – or his granny."

Sir Alex on former United centre half Steve Bruce

Player Power

"Look at Pele. He was a very aggressive attacker as well who could look after himself. So can Rooney. There are similarities. But he is white, completely white."

The manager ensures we don't mix the Brazil legend up with Wayne Rooney

"Cristiano declined to celebrate his goal. Which is just as well, because I would have strangled him. There were no issues with him at all. He's a very nice boy."

Ferguson after former player Cristiano Ronaldo scored the winner for Real Madrid against United in 2013

FERGIE TIME

"If I was putting Roy Keane out there to represent Manchester United on a one against one, we'd win the Derby, the National, the Boat Race and anything else."

On Roy Keane

"He's said to me half a dozen times, 'I played centre-half for the school you know'. I said, 'Yes, but not against Didier Drogba'."

On Wayne Rooney

"I have told him if he manages six by the end of the season, I'll give him £50 for a new haircut!"

He challenges Rafael to double his goal tally

Player Power

"That was a marriage made in hell. The minute [Ruud] Van Nistelrooy signed his new contract, it was a certainty he was leaving here. His one idea was to go to Real Madrid."

Fergie fell out with the Dutchman

"When [Peter] Schmeichel raises his voice, the walls shudder."

On the giant goalkeeper

"What I know for certain is that I'd rather have Gary Neville in my team than some kind of cold fish."

Erm!

FERGIE TIME

FERGIE V WENGER

FERGIE TIME

"He has no experience of English football. He's come from Japan. And now he's into English football and he is now telling everybody in England to organise their football. I think he should keep his mouth shut."

Sir Alex is angry at Arsene Wenger for opposing the extension of the league season with United facing their last four games in eight days

"They say he's an intelligent man, right? Speaks five languages! I've got a 15-year-old boy from the Ivory Coast who speaks five languages!"

He takes a swipe at the Arsenal boss

Fergie v Wenger

"In the tunnel Wenger was criticising my players, calling them cheats, so I told him to leave them alone and behave himself. He ran at me with his hands raised saying, 'What do you want to do about it?' To not apologise for the behaviour of the players to another manager is unthinkable. It's a disgrace, but I don't expect Wenger to ever apologise... he's that type of person."

Ferguson after a 2-0 Old Trafford win over the Gunners in 2005

"They got away with murder. What the Arsenal players did was the worst I have witnessed in sport."

After the Battle of Old Trafford in 2003

FERGIE TIME

"He was livid. His fists were clenched. I was in control, I knew it. Anyway, the next thing I knew I had pizza all over me."

Sir Alex on Arsene Wenger and 'Pizzagate' after his United team ended Arsenal's 49-game unbeaten run

"He never comes for a drink with the opposing manager after matches. He's the only manager in the Premiership not to do so. It is a tradition here. It would be good for him to accept the tradition."

Fergie on Wenger turning down a glass of wine with him

Fergie v Wenger

"Arsene Wenger disappoints me when he is reluctant to give credit to Manchester United for what we have achieved. And I don't think his carping has made a good impression on other managers in the Premiership."

Ferguson on Wenger in 2000

"They are scrappers who rely on belligerence – we are the better team."

He attacks Arsenal after they claim the 2001/02 league title with a 1-0 win at Old Trafford

FERGIE TIME

"Arsene Wenger is somebody I'd like to get to know better. People who do know him tell me he is a good man but I don't suppose I'll ever find out myself. He seems to pull the shutters down when you meet him and he never has a drink with you after the game."

Ferguson's observation in 2003

"It's petty. I can't think why he has said it. But I think it's about making him look great again. You know: I'm the great Arsene Wenger!"

Fergie responds to Arsene Wenger's claim that United have a problem with stamina

Fergie v Wenger

"I think it's obvious Arsenal have been doing deals with the FA for years. Look at the number of times they've got off with charges outside of the 50-odd sendings-off they have had under Wenger. I think they have been up 10 times before the FA and have got off with eight of those. It's remarkable, very remarkable. We hope we win titles without anybody's help."

Fergie's rant at Arsenal which he had to apologise for to avoid an FA charge

"It's just the two of us. We'll probably ride out in the sunset together."

Sir Alex reckons he and Wenger will end up becoming the best of friends

FERGIE TIME

SAY THAT AGAIN?

FERGIE TIME

"When an Italian tells me it's pasta on the plate I check under the sauce to make sure. They're the inventors of the smokescreen."

Ferguson is wary of doing business with the Italians

"I said it in pre-season. In fact, I may have said it before the season started."

So that's pre-season then?

"Of all the many qualities a good team must possess, the supreme essential for me is penetration. And Eric brought the can opener."

On Eric Cantona

Say That Again?

"It was just handcuffs at dawn."

Sir Alex mixes up his metaphors

"Sometimes you look in a field and see a cow. You think it's a better cow than the one you see in your field. It never really works out that way."

Fergie on why Wayne Rooney should remain at United

"As with every young player he's only 18."

Sir Alex makes a fair point!

"It's a conflict of parallels."

OK then!

FERGIE TIME

"I think Glaswegians and the people in the west of Scotland grow up in a different climate."

The manager knows his weather

"The real friend is the one who walks through the door when the others are putting on their coats to leave."

Fergie gets his coat

"Whether dribbling or sprinting, Ryan can leave the best defenders with twisted blood."

Sir Alex on Ryan Giggs

Say That Again?

"If we can play like that every week, we'll get some level of consistency."
Is that right?

"That lad must have been born offside."
Sir Alex on Filippo Inzaghi

"The players couldn't pick each other out. They said it was difficult to see their teammates at distance when they lifted their heads. It was nothing to do with superstition."
On the notorious grey kit that was changed at half-time against Southampton in 1996

FERGIE TIME

"If Chelsea drop points, the cat's out in the open. And you know what cats are like – sometimes they don't come home."

Ferguson the cat man

"I tell the players that the bus is moving. This club has to progress. And the bus wouldn't wait for them. I tell them to get on board."

Sir Alex the driver

"The birds are whistling here and the sparrows are waking up at Stamford Bridge coughing."

Fergie's view on Chelsea

Say That Again?

"I'm going to tell you the story about the geese which fly 5,000 miles from Canada to France. They fly in V-formation but the second ones don't fly. They're the subs for the first ones. And then the second ones take over – so it's teamwork."

The geese?

"You can play chess for about 10 hours and still lose, know what I mean?"

Erm, no...

"The lads ran their socks into the ground."

How could this be?

FERGIE TIME

Printed in Great Britain
by Amazon